Credo

Mervyn Linford
Credo

Credo published in the United Kingdom in 2017
by Mica Press

Leslie Bell, 47 Belle Vue Road, Wivenhoe, Colchester, Essex CO7 9LD

www.micapress.co.uk | books@micapress.co.uk

ISBN 978-1-869848-14-9

Copyright © Mervyn Linford 2017

The right of Mervyn Linford to be identified as the author of this work has been asserted by him in accordance with the Copyright, Designs and Patents Act of 1988.
All rights reserved.

Acknowledgements:

The author wishes to thank the editors of the following publications in which some of these poems first appeared:

From the City to the Coast - Poetry in Practice
Curlew Magazine
French Literary Review
Southend Poetry
Acumen
Twelve Rivers - Journal of the Suffolk Poetry Society
Poetry Aloud - poetryaloud.org.uk
NatureWriting.com

Contents

Sunset (Creeksea) 1
Wet & Westerly (Bradwell Waterside) 2
Indistinguishable (Marsh Road - Burnham on Crouch) 4
November the Fifth - Two Tree Island 5
Bait Digger - Two Tree Island - Christmas Morning 6
Credo - Two Tree Island 7
Peewits and Planets 8
Bait Digging 9
Black-tailed Godwits - Mersea Island 10
Inchoate 11
Inspiration 13
Seascape in November 14
The Swale 15
Gothic - Thames Estuary 16
Optical Illusions (Flanders) 17
Messages 18
The Flea Pit 19
I.M. Patrick and Thomas Barnett 21
Time's Cold Aspect 23
Through the Leaves - Through the Branches 24
Golden Shower 25
Hair-raising 26
Song & Dance 27
Small Talk 28
Woodies 29
An Old Man's Fancy 30
DNA 27% 31
Dawn in Betws y Coed 32
Greggs - Sudbury 33
Il Est Né 34
Autumn Bond 36
Home Goal 37
Essex Skippers 38
Epiphany at Chartres 39
Landscape in November 40

Teasels – Long Melford 41
Cache..42
Esox Lucius..43
Midnight Flood 44
Common Land – Sudbury...45
Draw...46
Mill Pool 49
Down..51
Nature Study 52
September Dawn – Sudbury..53
Before the Snow 54
Soundless 55
Words for Winter 56
Black Headed Gulls – Sudbury..57
Spate – Liston Mill – River Stour..58
Double Deeps 59
Miracle 60
Castle Park – Clare – Suffolk...61
The Croft, St Gregory's and the Stour....................................62

Sunset (Creeksea)

Where the tide
has spilled across the road
puddles reflect the sky:

sky and the rusted purslane
    and the moon –
that cold and skull-like, gibbous
smudge of white that speaks of stars.

    Here on green-encrusted ropes
bladder wrack is black and hung awry
where water once upheld it to the light
       in silver strands.

The double deeps hold wings
    as cormorant fly

and on the river's misted other side
where seals and mullet meet and multiply
    the sun explodes.

Wet & Westerly (Bradwell Waterside)

There is not much definition:
grey sky, grey sea,
and a misted ambience.

A curlew stalks the tide -
is twice the size
of three attendant redshank.

Its plaintive cry
follows a skein of geese
then fades to gutturals.

This is the least of places
    called sublime
and yet it holds my senses

and my mind - my seasoned heart.
It is home to so many migrants:
waders, geese and ducks,

visitors from the far north -
marking time; wintering.
How different here from the Steppes,

the Tundra, the Arctic Circle.
Here it is wet and westerly -
the rain drives across the estuary

    in sheets
and light is in abeyance.
No midnight sun

brightens this dull November:
this sense of isolation
that deprives -

and yet enlightens.
I am alive to this
to platinum and mercury and pewter

where seagulls carve the airways
    and contrive
to find a meaning.

INDISTINGUISHABLE (MARSH ROAD - BURNHAM ON CROUCH)

Just the wind's breath
and the patter of the rain.

Little else
save brown fields
as far as the eye can see

and three electric cables
looping towards infinity.

This is Essex at its level best –
    marshes, a few trees,
        sporadic hedgerows.

Here, cloud and sea
are indistinguishable:

lapwings pepper the fields
and rooks in black battalions

float over lonely farms.
    Who could love
        such a landscape –

such an isolate
expressionless terrain

where waves and furrows
    meet in monochrome
        and time is silent?

November the Fifth - Two Tree Island

This light is blinding:

the sea - like silver foil -
refracts the fallen sunlight from a tide
   that sears the mudflats.

How can November burn?

The geese - like flying sparks -
sputter with the gutturals of autumn
   and light a fuse.

All is pyrotechnics:

names like *Brock's* and *Standard
   Wizard* and *Pain's*
flare - like the coruscations of the sea -
   and flocks of dunlin.

Bait Digger – Two Tree Island – Christmas Morning

Three ships – not exactly:
Leigh Ray and Tewkes Creek
wind their grey and convoluted track
between the Christmas banks of mud and sand
where bladder wrack and eelgrass frame the day
   in wreaths of darkness.

One isolated figure, dressed in black,
squelches through the ooze and seems to say
that loneliness is human and the lack of winter light.

A curlew flutes, and sound, its sad refrain,
floats across the sandbanks and the flats
to where the sun, a star in all but name,
illuminates a trinity of gulls
   between the clouds.

Credo – Two Tree Island

Here, the tide is immediate:
it ebbs and flows uncannily –
swamps, or is high and dry,
before the mind can register
   its meanings.

A redshank holds my eye
and I perceive the ooze
that once was water
as my dominion.

These phases of the moon and all that changes –
that alters with its neaps and springs and slacks
defines I think my temporal derangement
   and all that's lunar.

The geese are loud and black
and where they fly in loose unwritten lines
across the silent silver of the flats –
   there lies my madness.

I am a child of this place:
a wader without wings –
a mullet with warm lungs;
a whistling, featherless, widgeon.

A curlew flutes its isolate amen
and I must choose between the sane horizons
and these religious littorals of light
   that fuel my fervour.

Peewits and Planets

   As it darkens
the lights beyond the saltings
scintillate – like stars.

The sky, though cloudless,
is pink and blue and green –
portentous it seems of frost
   and even fog.

A skein of brent geese
   unravels
and settles on the mudflats.

You can hear them barking
   as curlew bubble
      and lapwing pitch
their piercing, high, nomenclature.

No stars, no moon, as yet –
we await the reflective ones
that circle the ecliptic and the spheres.

Mars, Mercury, Jupiter,
you can hear them if you listen.

They sound like gulls
that glitter in the frost
or widgeon in the fogbanks
   out to sea –
webbed and whistling.

Bait Digging

Alone in the vastness of the ooze
   he digs for ragworm:

the sky and the far horizon
are for him the world's entirety –

sapphire and silver
   the ambience.

The scent of mudflats and mussel beds
follows the tortuous journey of the creek
   and light's slow ebb.

He pauses from his toil
   – straightens –
assesses his surroundings.

From compass point to compass point
the isolate dimensions of the tide
resonate with suction and the cries
   of gulls and curlew.

BLACK-TAILED GODWITS – MERSEA ISLAND

Three godwits –
three black-tailed godwits
standing at the tide's full edge.

One – on one leg:
head tucked in beneath a wing –

   snoozes.

The others – busier with worms and molluscs –
and all such things secreted in the ooze beneath their feet

   are almost black

silhouetted in the heat of late September
and the sun-shot, glittering, shatter of the sea
   in smithereens.

Bladder wrack and eelgrass
seep into the senses with the smell
of oyster smacks and cockle spits and brine

and early, but expected, from the east
the darkening skeins of those dark-bellied geese
who write their cursive script across a sky as wide as winter.

INCHOATE

Why do I sit here
  – alone –
looking at the sea?

I have you I love
and a few friends
and yet I need this space
  – this solitude –

I like the idea of horizons:
something beyond
  – uncertainty –
a world without the facts.

Emptiness is where it starts
wide vistas – distances

blue sky and blue sea
touching each other's void
failing to communicate.

A black headed gull
like the beginnings of form
worries the width of summer
  with a word

the gift – if that's the term –
  for such as language.

Perhaps if I stay here
  long enough
after the sun has set
beneath the stars

my love of isolation
and the darkness
will parse infinity.

Until then the moon and I
must muse on our dual insanity

and she   if she it is

  - beneath the tide -

will shine at depth
like some unwritten poem -
beautiful but fathomless.

Inspiration

Inspiration comes and it goes:
one day a wing, the next a flower or a leaf,
and then, something other.

Today it is Peewit Island
and the geese, or eponymous plovers
flickering over the saltings, the marina and the creek
like semaphore.

The view towards Mersea on one side
and Tollesbury on the other is grey, and yet,
aesthetically inclined

as a Thames, heeled-over barge, under full, magnificent sail
cleaves the pewter wavelets of the tide
on its journey seawards.

The scarcely audible tinkling of metal shrouds
against metal masts adds a resonant treble
to the fluted ground-bass of waders
and the harsh, yet evocative,
gutturals of overwintering geese.

A rook on a post, half green with seaweed,
half black with tar, angles its slick and opportunist eye
on the lookout for *fruits de mer* and other saline delicacies
and its stuttering staccato of a voice
echoes the reverberating shrouds and the rain's
irrepressible tattoo.

Seascape in November

My vehicle is buffeted by the wind:
here in the car park on Mersea Island facing west
where the tide lapping at the level of the land is as grey
    as the sky's inclemency.

Yachts – moored or at anchor – ride the increasing
whiteness of the waves, like horses over Becher's Brook
only to slam and flounder helplessly on the other side.

Memories of men who dredged for oysters
and lived out their J Class lives under the ensign
with pride and a sense of superior purpose
are forgotten now as children freed at last
    from digital enslavement
dangle their bacon fat and rind for the green
and bubbling surprise of astounded shore crabs.

Migratory birds: passerines, waders and wildfowl
ignore the shifting borders that infiltrate our minds
and the annals of history to settle down
across the thoughtless saltings and the creeks
to feed and further instinct and survival.

The rain comes on and slants across the Strood
as I regain the mainland's other side
where legions marched and Boudicca defied all Roman rule
    as far as distant London

and I who've lived with Essex as my guide
beneath the seaxe of this old Saxon Kingdom
inscribe these words despairing of all tribes
and thank the gods of lavender and purslane
for all the cold indifference of their eyes
    and what they've seen.

The Swale

Out there beyond the Yantlet,
the Middle Grounds, the Medway and Sheppy,

    we find the Swale.

Wider than your average creek and less sinuous
it cleaves the earth between the sea and downs
and leads the way to Thanet and the dead.

Before the ingenuity of man
with buoys and charts
to lead us up the Thames

this corridor of ooze and pewter tides
saw Roman galleys hauling flocks of gulls
without the curse of keels to run aground
    before Londinium.

Celts and Romans,
Saxon and Dane,
Jutes and Normans:

This route has seen them all
and here this Sunday morning in the sun
with mist across the mudflats and the geese
whose own migrations teach us how to wonder and surmise
    I preach again the primacy of words.

This ink that flows across the written page
as I, although inspired, start to ebb
will capture time like flounders in a net

and history – yes yours – and even mine
will be the sounds of seabirds in the west
as Venus sinks toward Canary Wharf
    then fades and founders.

GOTHIC - THAMES ESTUARY

Out there – somewhere – beyond the mist,
Ray Gut and the mudflats,
I can hear the widgeon:

can hear the bell clanging on a rusted buoy -
its counterpoint to the whistling, webbed
expression of the sea –
hollow and muted
and spectral.

Out there – in the cloisters and the corridors of grey
where a curlew, like the logos in the void,
echoes through the nave of this cold sky
with sadness or the sanctity of stone
    in dawn's cathedral.

Optical Illusions (Flanders)

Flanders is wet, very wet:
the flat fields are full of sky –
of sailing clouds and blue, unbounded spaces.

A thousand gulls float and flap and fly
and their screeching voices climb ever skyward
    like demented angels.

    A heron stands alone –
a statue being doubled and defined
by mystic waters.

Everything here is twice:
two by two the whole reflected world
inclines the eye the senses and the mind

    to something other.
In one divided moment out of time
a gull descends – and rises – and I'm blind to what is real.

Messages

History is a scar:
this fingertip remembers
glass and nettles –

  a sprawling.

Saturday morning flicks,
elm trees, Station Lane,
   the market.

These were the things
that found me
in the undergrowth.

Stung from knees to shoulders:
a gash on the middle finger –
   blood oozing.

Cuts and a cloudless sky,
cabbage-whites, bees,
   slowworms.

Messages come in bottles
  – or so it seems –
 even broken ones.

Stitches and Calamine Lotion
  eased my suffering
    the tearfulness.

I can still remember the birdsong:
the delicate veins of nettles and ephemera –
the kestrel
         hovering.

The Flea Pit

Saturday morning flicks
   why bother?

The noise was abysmal
   crazy kids
running in all directions

everything imaginable
thrown into the
projector's beams
usherettes shushing
girls screeching

and poor Flash Gordon
trying his best to be heard
as he faced the unearthly terrors
of space and the evil Ming

the Bash Street Kids
were nothing compared
   with this lot

sneaking in through the exit
smoking in the toilets
letting off squibs and tuppenny cannons

'Hey Pancho' – 'Hey Cisco'
   'How!'

Where was Hopalong Cassidy
when you needed him?

Someone to corral the unruly mob –
High Noon in the flea pit.

I remember the Three Stooges
the sadistic celluloid slapstick
as we rushed to avoid
the National Anthem.

I slapped my irreverent arse
and galloped all the way home
    'Hey Tonto'
        'Hi-Yo Silver'
            'Kemo Sabe'.

I.M. Patrick and Thomas Barnett

How cold it was at Thiepval:
    somewhere in these January fields
        lie the bones of two young men.

Two brothers – two Irish boys
born in England but Irish
killed on the same day in the same battle.

This, they say, is the largest
British war memorial in the world

and it is large, very large -

it has to be 72,000 men: British, Irish,
South African, died here, and for what?
    You tell me.

Ellen Dalton from Tralee, Kerry
died in 1914 and never saw the telegrams
written with the blood of her sons.

Her husband, Michael from Cork,
my great grandfather died in 1919.

Was it from heartbreak
    or bitterness
so close to 1916 in Ireland.

Did my grandmother cry for her brothers?
I did – today, here in the bitter wind
where their two cold names are carved
into colder stone on this grand memorial –
    are frozen in time.

Here, *en hiver*, to raise their temperature
and their spirits, they had a kick about
    at Christmas –
shared a carol or two with the enemy
and saw *les sapins de noel* lit with candles.
Their Epiphany was different:
the manifestation was that of ice and snow –
their *cadeaux* rats and trench foot.

Gifts are still unearthed by the local farmers:
not gold or frankincense or myrrh
but another century's deadly ordinance –
    shells, grenades, bullets.

My hands are frozen
as I watch the crows
growing fat on carrion.

Everything here symbolises death
    and as I walk towards the car
        over the gravel that rattles
            in so many ghostly throats

        the last few desperate leaves
          clinging to the gnarled, arthritic branches
      catch the razor edge of this cruel wind
and disseminate – like sadness.

Time's Cold Aspect

Here in the light
beneath the leaves:

– few and spare –

that stay or fathom
as they will,

   I wait.

And where are you –
you who have colours
like the leaves,

autumn tints
and wintering remarks
that wither like

the flowers of the sun
and time's cold aspect?

I am undone
without your whispering words –
your soft as silk

persuasions of the mind
that tilt my longing heart
towards the snow

and love's refusals.

THROUGH THE LEAVES – THROUGH THE BRANCHES

The light penetrates the leaves –
not quite golden but lemony or yellow.

The leaves I think are hornbeam
  maybe beech.

I'm no arboriculturist
  and yet I preach
    the primacy of trees

my favourite flowers.

Would you believe
the hours that I've spent
beneath the branches' bifurcating eaves

watching the sunlight –
watching the moon?

Xylem and phloem
have found me on my knees –
not to mention photosynthesis.

Dryads are one thing
chlorophyll another –
  myth and science
sow their different seeds

and even in winter
  leafless and laden
    with a skin of snow

I still can see the planets and the stars
held after midnight, like the fruits of darkness.

Golden Shower

When I was young
  very young:

when the sun was made of gold
  and not of helium -

when hydrogen was something
  yet unheard of

and photons touched my sight
  without a meaning

  you were unknown

and yet that sense
of oneness that we strive for -
that all-embracing energy of love
was there in every starling, every stone
  and every season.

And even now when reason intervenes
between each cruel event and your blue eyes
I still can see your heart in every flower
  in every star.

And why should I
when time repeats each hour
believe in less than beauty as a truth

when we like autumn leaves
    in golden showers
        renew love's soil.

Hair-raising

There is pollarding and there is butchery:
These five assaulted limes beside the wall
   are more than stunted.

Their thin, upstanding branches
have all the swank of Yankee crewcuts:

longer perhaps - but just as shocking.

Perhaps they've seen a ghost -
the spectre of some crazed arborist,
wide-eyed, chainsaw in hand,
   grinning manically.

In spring there will be an improvement -
a green amelioration of the leaves
hiding the traces of hirsute barbarity.

Perhaps a blackbird will come -
will perch on this verdant *bouffant*
singing its songs of Sweeny and Seville
   with mandibles - like scissors.

Song & Dance

Listening to the rooks –
the harsh yet welcome calls
   that augur spring

I think of all the years
and how they pass
between us and the glances
   and our lives.

We are still here
the two of us
in love

as songbirds sing
St Valentine's refrain
and cherries blossom.

And what will last they say
   is love alone

but I proclaim
no echo like the thrush
as on we dance towards
   that fateful day

where darkness snuffs
the snowdrop and the rose
and rooks are silent.

Small Talk

So small this blue tit:
a speck of fallen sky
gilded by sunlight.

How it scurries
　mouse-like
through the branches

pecking at nothing

or nothing to my eyes
blind as they are
to nature's deeper mysteries.

Bugs and chrysalides
hide beneath bark
and in crevices

and the blue tit
knows these secrets
　instinctively.

I have to read, look,
listen and learn

but he in the hands
of the first Big Bang
and the clock's un-sprung
　fecundity

glitters with the knowledge
　of the stars
　　and the sun's soliloquy.

Woodies

Why does this big fat ring-dove
   remind me of a bishop –

Is it that paintings in the past depicted them
with after dinner port and thick cigars

whilst lesser mortals
scratched about for crumbs
and felt unworthy?

They certainly seem pompous
      even proud

      and 'humble access'
        – well –

there are no vows or sacraments enough
to keep these plump columbiformes
      – we trust –
from business at the table or the trough.

An Old Man's Fancy

I am happy with the spring:
even in age my fancy turns to love
as blackbirds sing and swallows haunt the wires –
    like quotes or quavers.

You are to me still light and all those things
that bud and bloom along the river's edge
like kingcups in the margins and the strings
    of glistening spawn.

We chime with nature's thoughts, if thoughts they are,
as great tits ring the changes in the woods
and bluebells and anemones surpass
the cuckoo's fearful chant and all that stings –
    like bees or nettles.

DNA 27%

So this is where my ancestors came from:
here on this rain-soaked isle
where green is both the symbol and the fact
   of pride and purpose.

This dairy farm beneath Atlantic winds
where industry and commerce make demands
   on Celtic legends.

Samhain is when the cattle and the sheep
can still command a price when they're preserved
to feed far more than leprechauns and fairies
   in Patrick's kingdom.

Michael and Ellen found the living hard
and made their way to London's 'golden' streets
   to starve in England.

Two of their boys were sentenced by the Somme
to die together side by side in France
   for king and country.

This is the split:
    the stick that's cleft
       in my divided being –

more English than Irish

   and yet

here I sense the anguish and regret
as my two antecedents left their hearts
to die and lose their children and their dreams
   in Cruel Britannia.

Dawn in Betws y Coed

If you're looking for magic:
that sense of something other –
   then look no further.

See where the Conwy steps between the rocks –
touches the gravel redds with icy feet
and dashes its wizened hair on banks and boulders.

This is a dawn where dippers dredge the light
for caddis grubs and other watery fare
   in silent pools.

Oak and alder shade and over-stare
the river's restless gouging of the rocks
where aeons and the instant come to share
   this cleft of sunlight.

Note: redds are spawning nests formed by female salmon using their tails to dig into the gravel at the bottom of the river.

GREGGS – SUDBURY

Gainsborough's statue
stands before the church.

St Peter's, still consecrated
but used for farmers' markets,
fairs and meetings – rarely services.

    Nevertheless
    atheism cannot compete –

this edifice of higher things and art
dominates the *Nationwide* and *Greggs*
where juggernauts fork either left or right
for Chelmsford and the Kingdom of St Edmund.

Sitting here
   before the dawn
      waiting for tea and toast

I think of Little Cornard and the Stour:
of Constable's altar pieces –
of Gainsborough's love of 'landskip'
when forced into portraiture.

How trivial it all seems:
all the dreams I had –
all the beliefs when I was young.

Gainsborough holds a palette
   made of bronze

yet even so the traffic is redeemed
by skies of scumbled light – and this red sun –
that rises into Suffolk's holy frame
   like love's impasto.

Il Est Né

It's that time again:
that time when Christ is almost tangible –
when virgin births and worshipping Magi
are as real as the vividness of our own imaginations.

Tinsel and baubles have their charms admittedly
but fail to assuage the need for something deeper –
    less superficial.

Even I, cynic that I am in old age,
respond to the old traditional ways –
the carols, the memory jerkers.

Today – driving between Halstead and Sudbury
listening to Annie Lennox and her 'Christmas Cornucopia'
Fallow deer parade their festive credentials beneath the trees –

trees that are decked for yuletide
with their multi-coloured late November leaves
and hanging fruits, for wassailers and mummers.

The holly is red with berries
and the ivy with its evergreen intentions
clings as it coils under balloons of mistletoe.

Hiatus or stasis – I'm just not certain –
but time is all time for me at this
    inexplicable moment.

Childhood and age hold hands across the body's frail divide
    and the old excitements reassert themselves.

Il est né le divin enfant – is it true?

Annie says so with her Christmas voice

as sweet as Christmas candy, chocolate coins, or tangerines:

Il est né – she sings –

    il est né

        il est né

            il est né.

Autumn Bond

A pair of kestrels, hovering, hunting, flying together:
are they a pair, now in mid-November -
   already bonded?

Waiting for spring and the nascent year's
   attempts at fecundity?

Here in the chill and silence by the Stour
It's hard to think of cowslips and the glare
   as loud as lark song.

Perched in a tree denuded by the weather
this twosome share whatever is the way
   of fish and falcons.

I too am paired in partnership
   - a lover -
and that young girl once fair and now so grey

still moves me like the leaves and that one feather
that falls and floats through sunlight and the air
   that's still unfathomed.

Home Goal

I think we formed an understanding
   - eventually -

Before he died, before that heart of hardness
softened a little and broke, we, father and prodigal son
spoke of subjects other than his disappointment in me
and my fears and bitterness towards his coldness
    and severity.

I think I could have pretended to enjoy cricket
   and even football
and he may well have deigned to parley
   about angling and natural history.

He loved his garden and his wife
   if little else
and although I loathe the spade, the hoe, the mower,
I'm very fond of trees and shrubs and flowers -

   common ground
      perhaps.

Too late, unfortunately,
a blood clot through his heart and through his lungs
killed both him and any chance of a real
   and lasting rapprochement.

Now when I look at dahlias and chrysanthemums

   - his favourite flowers -

they seem far more funereal than they should
and those horned and horrendous earwigs
that strike fear - or even worse - in other people
   are somehow celebratory.

Essex Skippers

Trying to remember now those fields
where as a child I stared into the sky
amongst the flowers
    is never easy.

I can see in my mind's eye the vetches
and the willow herb and poppies
but time has taken something from the light
    that was my vision.

I cannot see or feel such fleeting things
as burnet moths or lizards or the wings
    of Essex skippers.

Images it seems are not enough
I need the actual touch that words can't bring
of butterflies between the cupping hands

whose gentle tickling beat is like a heart
that leaves behind a powder and the mark
    of all ephemera.

Epiphany at Chartres

Phillipe Lejeune:
a name unknown to me
until stopping by chance
at the Collégiale Saint-André
    in Chartres.

And there to astound in an *exposition d'été*
were depictions in oil of the Jewish
    and Christian Testaments.

Ancient and Modern is the phrase
where the figurative and the abstract
join their devotional hands in painterly magnificence.

This artist, equally known for his stained glass
manages it seems that rare mélange of geometry and colour

and whether it's Moses on the mount,
    the Virgin's immaculate Nativity
        or the Three Wise Men kneeling in adoration

Like the labyrinth in Notre Dame Cathedral
each brush stoke is a pilgrimage in paint
that moves towards the centre where we start
    and where we end.

LANDSCAPE IN NOVEMBER

The willows beside the river are showing the effects of age –
the branches that have snapped are lying at angles
to the uprights and autumn's yellowing foliage.

It could be a painting by Constable
here along the River Stour at Liston in Essex.

Long Melford church, one of Suffolk's wool churches
    – cathedrals more like –
looks out across the water meadows and grazing cattle.

Timeless indeed, apart from me that is,
sitting here in the car and listening to Christmas music
by the Albion Band on a memory stick plugged in to my
    on-board computer.

If there was a pear tree hereabouts
no doubt there would be a partridge for accompaniment -

but today I'll make do with this raucous
and resplendent pheasant escaped from both the shotgun
and the greetings card to strut like some exotic Indian prince
in the faded sepia landscape of a sunless and half-remembered empire.

Teasels – Long Melford

The teasels have outgrown the bulrushes –
nearly as tall as a man they stand their prickly ground
between the river and the water meadows.

A charm of goldfinches

   – how apt –

defy this apparent barbarity
to feed and tintinnabulate
   like tiny bells.

I'm on tenterhooks as I think about the past –
the wealth acquired through sheep and wool
as these latter day survivors of a craft
   nap our November skies.

   Long Melford church
more cathedral than parish focal point,
stares our across the corduroy of the fields –
   newly ploughed.

Lavenham Blues, Kersey Cloth, Linsey Woolsey:
the green baize of the water meadows
waits in trepidation for the floods
   – the winter spates –
while the warp and weft of pheasants, rooks, and fieldfares,
weave their autumn tapestry of sound with faded threads.

CACHE

Just a week:
a week of autumn wind
  and autumn rain

  and the trees –
the trees beside the Stour's
up-brimmed meanderings are almost bare.

Here and there
like gilt uncounted coins
a cache of residual leaves detach themselves
and glitter down the air this cold November.

The sulphur smell of last night's pyrotechnics
            – hangs –
like the kestrel's predatory stare above the meadows

and greyness – though it borders on despair –
is cleaved apart by sun-shafts and the glare
of light across a spate that brims and boils
  like molten gold.

Esox Lucius

Concentric is the moment of the pike:
and then the shards and splinters that explode
as fish and fry hurl heavenwards - subside -
    in rafts of silver.

How calm this river glides:
the willow-herb, the willows, autumn light -
where green as jade the water holds the sun
    in moistened palms.

Tooth and claw - and even mandibles:
nature's law is here despite our dreams
as bloodlike delves the evening close to dusk
    and foxes bark.

The darkness will imbibe the risen moon:
will swallow whole the rictus of a scream
where roach and bream and gudgeon swim like sparks
    and *esox* glimmers.

Midnight Flood

We have times:
times when the river breaches winter's bounds
and meadowland is saturate with stars.

Is that the moon that sounds without a sound
where somnolent the fishes wear their shrouds
    of liquid silver?

Times when the hooting owl - aloft and loud -
stares at the midnight deeps with golden eyes
    and harsh intentions.

Here where the darkness suddenly astounds
with all the stainless ambience of steel
    and molten swans.

Common Land – Sudbury

This January light is low and soft
and where it earths between the sunlit clouds
    the grass is mellow.

The oldest grazed and cared-for common land
lies crazed by every facet of the Stour
    that gleams and glitters.

How many feet have trod these ancient ways
that curve between two counties and the crests
    of subtle hills?

I add as best I can my pilgrim heart
along these paths inhabited by swans
    and flights of mallard.

So many wings where Zeus becomes an angel
and Leda with her Labradors absconds
    from thoughts of time.

Draw

All week the pike evaded me:
submerged beside a log
close to my feet
he waited.

Whenever I caught a fish
disgorged and released it –
he would pounce.

Would roll – himself a living log –
open his maw at a lunge
and swallow the titbit
    whole.

He – or perhaps she –
    being so large
exhausted all my tactics –
    my slick ideas.

This was wisdom
    writ large –

an old tooth-ridden head
on a long evolving body –
    laughing almost.

On the last day
after ledger and float
and dead-bait –

after revolving spoons
and surface plugs
    and divers

I was at a loss.
One last chance.

An hour before dusk
snap tackle and a sprat
dangled in front of it
like a silver puppet.

This time – instinct
outwitted wisdom.

He – or she – snatched
at the shimmering bait
 and was on.
First the deep plunge –
the rod at full bend
and the clutch screaming.

Then the tail-walk –
the sunset splintered water
all thrash and crystal.

The fish was big –
a swirling length
of sheer primeval power

testing my wits and my nerve
as I drew it ever closer
to the net.

The prize was
within my grasp:

half in and half out
of the waiting mesh
it see-sawed for
an infinite second
spat out the hooks
and was gone.

I was at once bereft
and yet satisfied.

The combat had been
  honourable –
the result, a draw.

I shrugged my human
shoulders and smiled.

At the other end
of the evolutionary scale –
deep in the green
and unfathomable
  depths
I imagined two
inscrutable eyes
looking upwards.

Mill Pool

It is warm for September
and the sun's seductive eye

– brazen for the time of year –

withers leaf and flower
   with a look
and kills composure.

The silence is too hot –
the ducks too amorous.

There is a fire in the hedgerows –
hops like burning lanterns

turn the old-man's-beard
      to drifts of smoke
            and cloud all reason.

The mill pool glimmers or glows –
is a raft of golden embers
      that conspire

            to stun or stifle.

Where is the frost:
the mist across the meadows –
   snowfall?

I need these stark anatomies –
   winter's bones.

         Then there is truth:
      no torrid looks –
no lascivious glances.

Only the barren
    background of existence –
        formless, elemental, frigid.

Down

There is so much swans' down
    along the margins of the mill pool
        that it looks as if snow or cat ice
            has formed in the warmth of early August.

How strange –
incongruous.

I have seen frozen lakes,
mill pools, rivers, canals,

    but this mix
        of ice and fire
           is exceptional.

Ring-doves unleash their syllables –
those summer sounds of heat and listlessness
that drop from the tops of willow trees and alders
    and breed monotony.

    Sometimes
after the clap of sudden wings:
    when tranquillity is broken
           and mindlessness is countered and confused –

feathers out of nowhere flake and fall
        to drift across the falsity of sequence
                and freeze perception.

Nature Study

Why would the chestnut
have a grazing line?

On this side of the mill pool
there are no cattle,
no roe deer, no fallow.

The willow tree's the same:
a horizontal plane of leaves
five feet or so above the ground –

    uncanny.

Nature has its ways I suppose:
doesn't tell us everything –
just nuances – intimations.

A tern is hovering

    head still

  a steady eye
piercing the water's surface.

The shoals of bleak or dace
    no more than I
      know
all of nature's secrets.

Their ignorance is shattered

    so is mine

where impact has no reverence for icons
and all my thoughts, reflections, and ideas
    are smithereens.

September Dawn – Sudbury

                September
        studies
autumn:

the water meadows disappear in mist
and cattle – as if spectres – are dissolved
    then reappear.

Trees full-leaved yet fading are resolved
to change the greenest countenance to grey
    and mix their meanings.

I cannot say exactly
    what is what –

things
    drift
        shift
            delete

and then discover
    new ideas.

What was isn't
what wasn't is.

This is September's instinct for confusion
where elderberries, plums,
especially sloes

exhibit blooms
        a silkenness
                a semblance

    that snares the mind.

Before the Snow

Today is breathless:
high clouds – more white than grey –
invest the sun with pallor, like the moon,
    and hint at snow.

The river's jade is ripple less and calm
and winter's take on centigrade confirms
    the east's intentions.

A blackbird chinks alarm
and leafless trees – like veins into the sky –
convey each icy corpuscle of thought
    to cells of crystal.

Soundless

In the background
the sound of the rushing weir –

otherwise – silence.

This is October's
answer to the dawn:

listen – nothing.

A duck in the mill pool
    dives
and another watery sound
ripples through the stillness –
the tranquillity.

Mist across the meadows
amputates alders:
leaves oaks in mid-air –
cuts cattle in half.

    Water again

condensing – cold –
    concise.

    The sun –
drunk on the liquids
of the leaching stars

opens a bloodshot eye

and the woken morning
accompanied by geese
in loud formation

yawns as it stretches
into light and leaf-fall.

Words for Winter

There is a chill that speaks of winter -
words that fall like leaves or shooting stars
as old Orion strides into the skies
   we call November.

There is a moon that rises through the mist
but even this reflection of the sun
   prefigures ice.

I walk across the bridge
and in the dark the only sound's the weir -
save my succeeding footsteps
   that remark
   on such a silence.

The frost is almost audible -
each crystal like a phoneme that replies
to all the cold assumptions of the night
   and thought's debacle.

Black Headed Gulls – Sudbury

The mews are noisy –
screeching, cacophonous.

What are they doing?

Perched on a wall
beside the mill pool
they vie for something –
perhaps ascendancy.

It looks like
king of the castle
the black headed gulls'
version of amusement –
their way of passing time.

The willow, of course, weeps

   as it would

knowing no more than I
any rhyme or reason.

Suffice to watch
   I suppose
this aspect of creation:

to see the dust of stars
somehow translated
to bone and feather –

to realise a joy
that's unexplained
and their estranged indifference
to my thoughts on god or science.

SPATE - LISTON MILL - RIVER STOUR

The willows weep into the flood, would stand,
if they could, knee-deep in the deluge.

An inch of rain in November and the land,
already saturate, spills its extravagance, its excesses,
    into the raging Stour.

    The torrents are treacherous –
    are Scylla and Charybdis.

This way and that maelstroms and eddies
obliterate the mill pool and the back streams
and what was once a reach of tranquil waters
    churns as it boils.

The water meadows imbibe their own nomenclature:
are drunk enough on autumn's potent brew
to welcome chub and pike and even barbel
into the tipsy dance and waltzing swirl
    of this cold soiree.

Tonight they forecast frost, severe frost:
cat ice will creep and cling to quiet edges,
    owls will hoot
and a firmament so deep and drenched with stars
will find itself reflected in the spate –

a vast unfathomed
    turbulence that's cast
        in sheets of moonlight.

Double Deeps

The day is alternation:
    cloud and sunshine –
        blue sky and drizzle.

I too am changeable:
    nature or nurture –
        Gemini or genetic?

I scry myself in the river
    and try to understand
        my dim reflection.

A blackbird sings its melancholy song
and I am deaf to its green accompaniment.

It flies between my image and the swans:
a semibreve, a crotchet, or a quaver
that fathoms down the thermocline of light
  on staves of darkness

    and I am dumb
to hold the sun-shot moment
that fills the mind with scales of golden rudd
  and glint refractions.

Miracle

The sun shatters on the mill pool:
rippling jade makes golden coruscations
and every drake is gilded and transformed
    to molten metal.

Who said that miracles don't happen –
that epiphanies and other forms of mystic revelation

    are dreams and wishes?

Here today the science of refraction
has touched in time both mind and metaphysics

and light with all its speed and waves and quanta
is particulate beneath the flaking gulls
    that gleam and glitter.

Castle Park – Clare – Suffolk

The Stour is narrow here:
it draws a charcoal line between the fields
where paper is the pulp of fallen snow
    and art is silence.

Sunlight and such vortices appear
across the river's pointillistic surface
    of stippled gold.

Rooks have spread their silhouetted pinions
and as they feather brushstrokes into air
the palette is restricted to the hush
    of white and water.

The Croft, St Gregory's and the Stour

There is silence
        then the silence
                that is dusk.

Here by the Croft
    as the Muscovy
        tuck their heads
           into their wings

and the setting sun
    lengthens the shadows
        over the greensward
           and the water meadows

    a blackbird starts to sing.

This is the song of Venus:
   the notes of the evening star
      that climb like golden quavers and belie
         the dark-supposed indifference of night

      where planets roam and comets lose their tails
    and Sudbury's ancient edifice of stone
looks out across the common land to scry
the silver-plated waters of the moon.

www.ingramcontent.com/pod-product-compliance
Lightning Source LLC
Chambersburg PA
CBHW042130100526
44587CB00026B/4240